Win From Within:

Success Starts With You

Nigel Norvell

Published by Books By Norvell™
An imprint of Kingdom Norvell LLC
www.booksbynorvell.com
info@booksbynorvell.com
First Edition, 2025
Printed in the United States of America
ISBN: 979-8-9940100-0-6

DEDICATION

To my nephew, this began as advice for you as you take your
first steps into adulthood.

To my daughters, you are my daily reminder of purpose and
pride.

To my nieces, I see your potential and your strength, and I want
you to know that your future is filled with promise.

To every young person pursuing success, whether you are in
high school, in college, or simply finding your way, you do not
need perfection. You need progress.

Keep learning, keep growing, and understand success begins
with you.

CONTENTS

ACKNOWLEDGMENTS

This book would not exist without the people who poured into me and helped me grow into the man I am today. To my wife and daughters, thank you for your patience, love, and inspiration. To my nephew, who sparked the idea for this book, thank you for reminding me why mentorship matters. To every Soldier, mentor, friend, and family member who challenged me, supported me, or believed in me, this is for you.

INTRODUCTION: WHY I WROTE THIS

Win From Within: Success Starts With You began as advice for my nephew, who recently started college. Watching him step into early adulthood made me think about the lessons I wish someone had shared with me at his age. While I know he was raised well, there are lessons that only experience can teach. Even though I did not go to college right after high school the way he did, I have seen what it takes to navigate the real world. It is not easy, and no one truly prepares you for the moments that shape you. I wanted to encourage him to stay focused early, build discipline, and most importantly, understand how to pursue success.

Adults often tell young people what to do, but we do not always explain why they should do it. After sending him long text messages filled with advice, I realized he was not the only young person trying to make sense of life. There are millions of students stepping into life after high school or college with very little direction. That is when I realized my advice could become something more, a message for anyone beginning their journey toward success.

My goal is simple. I want young readers to live without regret. That familiar feeling of wishing you had known earlier what you know now is something I hope to help them avoid. This book is not about perfection or pretending life is easy. It is about being prepared, staying disciplined, and learning from every experience, both good and bad. To me, success has never been about the spotlight or applause. It is the ability to say, I gave it my all. My biggest fear has never been failure. It has always been being unprepared. That feeling pushes me forward, and I hope it motivates you as well.

My nephew may have inspired this book, but I wrote it with my entire family in mind. My daughters and nieces are growing up in a world that moves quickly, one that often confuses success with attention. I want them to know that true success is built on character, effort, and peace of mind, not popularity or perfection. Much of what I share comes from my experience as a Soldier and leader. The Army taught me that discipline and preparation are not only military values. They are life skills. Whether you are putting on a uniform, walking into class, or showing up for work, the way you prepare shapes how far you will go.

As you read this, I encourage you to think about your own story. The goal is not to live like me or anyone else, but to recognize that you have what it takes to win from within. You already carry the blueprint. You simply need to believe in it. By the time you reach the end of this book, I want you to understand one thing above all else:

You can succeed!

You will succeed!

And it begins within you!

CHAPTER 1: UNDERSTAND YOUR WHY

"If you do not know why you are doing something, every obstacle becomes the reason to quit."

Knowing your why matters because it becomes the foundation for everything you do. If you do not have a reason, then why are you doing it? Is it for your family, a personal goal, or maybe to avoid returning to where you started? Everyone has a reason that shapes how they act, think, and move.

When I was eighteen, I had to learn this lesson for myself. My "why" back then was simple: do not be broke and do not fail. Looking back, it sounds simple, but during basic training it became one of the hardest periods of my life. I was away from home for the first time, surrounded by strangers yelling at me, and expected to perform every day under pressure. My dad was deployed to Iraq at the time, and I carried that with me constantly. I refused to let him down. My parents, my church family, and my hometown were all waiting for me to return as a Soldier. In my mind, there was no in between. I was either coming home a Soldier or coming home a failure.

Quitting was never an option. I woke up every morning thinking about my "why". I did not want to embarrass my family or myself. Even on the hardest days, I reminded myself that I could do it. I learned that I could flip a switch in my mind and push through anything. Not just survive it, but rise above it. That experience changed the way I saw myself forever.

As I grew older, my "why" developed. What began as do not be broke became I want to provide for my family. I also wanted to leave a legacy and be a continuation branch for my family tree. We started one way, but because of my choices and mindset, our story shifted. I continued to build on what my parents began. That is the power of understanding your "why". It grows as you do.

If someone asked me how to find their "why", I would tell them to approach it the same way they think about holding their breath underwater. The longer you stay under, the more your body demands air. You stop caring about anything else. You focus. You fight. You push through whatever is in front of you because you know you cannot live without that next breath. That same level of urgency is what your "why" should feel like. It is the force that keeps you moving when everything around you slows down.

If you still do not know your reason, ask yourself these questions:
1) What do I want most right now?
2) Why does it matter to me?
3) What happens if I quit?

Your honest answers are the beginning of your "why". Do not overthink it or try to make it sound impressive. Just be honest with yourself.

The biggest mistake people make is chasing someone else's "why". They see what others are doing and try to copy it, but that never lasts. Your reason must be personal. You will know it is real when it keeps you moving even on your hardest days. Once you find your reason, pursue what you need to make it a reality. Your "why" shapes who you are. It becomes part of your character and guides every decision you make moving forward.

Remember your reason.

Write it down.

Protect it.

Live by it.

If you do not stand for something, you will fall for anything.

Reflection Questions:
- What truly drives you to keep moving forward when things get tough?
- If someone asked you your "why" today, could you explain it clearly and confidently?
- Has your reason for success changed as you have grown older?
- What would it look like if you started living every day with your "why" in mind?

Once you understand your "why", the next step is shaping who you are through character, because your purpose means nothing if your actions do not align with it.

CHAPTER 2: CHARACTER

"Character is who you are when no one is watching."

Character is the combination of everything you have been through and what those experiences were designed to teach you. It is not something you show only when it is convenient, and it is not a mask you wear to look good. Character is what helps you navigate life when the path gets hard. It is who you are now, who you have been, and who you are becoming. It is the difference maker.

When you are young, hanging out with the wrong crowd can feel almost inevitable. Everyone is searching for where they fit in. But there comes a moment when your character sets you apart from the people around you. It might happen when your friends are about to do something questionable and, instead of inviting you, they look you in the eye and say, "Sit this one out."

That moment hits differently. You may have always sensed that you did not quite fit in with that energy but hearing them confirm it changes everything. It is their way of acknowledging you and avoiding putting you in a situation that would be out of character for you. It is not an insult. It is respect. They recognize that something about you is solid, that there is a line you will not cross. That is character.

Everyone has a moment like that when a choice could shift everything. Character is not about what you say you believe.

It is about what you do when your beliefs are tested. It is the quiet voice in your head that says, "This is not me," even when the crowd is loud.

Character shows up in everything you do. It is in your mannerisms, your thoughts, your effort, and how you treat people. Some people could never steal or lie; it is simply not in them. For others, it is normal behavior because that is what life taught them. Character can be developed. You can learn, grow, and choose differently. The choice is yours.

I once read, "Control your thoughts so your thoughts will not lead into action." We are judged by our actions, not by our thoughts. That is why character starts in the mind. The moment you start letting small things go unchecked, like excuses, bad habits, or selfish decisions, your foundation begins to crack.

Good character comes naturally when you understand yourself. It is who you are at your core. You can fake kindness, but real character cannot be faked. When someone tries to act genuine but it is not in them, everyone can tell. Think back to that kid who was told to "sit out." That is how it works. Their friends recognized their character even before they fully did.

Maintaining good character is simple once you accept it as part of who you are. It does not mean you will never make mistakes. It means you own up to them when you do. It means keeping your word, staying honest even when it is uncomfortable, and walking away from things that do not align with who you are.

Character connects directly to ambition. Your "why" gives you purpose, but your character defines how you chase it. If you are dishonest or selfish, your ambition will reflect that.

You might still succeed, but it will come at a cost. The difference between ambition and greed is intention.

If your "why" is pure and your character is solid, you do not need shortcuts. You move with confidence because you trust your process. You are not trying to outshine anyone. You are simply trying to outgrow who you used to be.

Character always comes before ambition because it defines your motive. Without it, drive becomes dangerous. When you know who you are, your ambition has direction. It builds instead of destroys.

You might not always get credit for your character, and that is okay. The world might overlook it, but life never does. Good character builds trust, and trust builds opportunities.

Keep showing up with character. Let your word mean something. Be the person people can count on. When you are grounded in who you are, you do not have to tell people you have character. They will already know.

Reflection Questions:
- When people describe you, what do you want them to say about your character?
- How have your experiences shaped who you are today?
- Are there habits or traits you know you need to improve?
- What does having strong character mean to you when no one is watching?

Once you understand your character, you can unlock your drive. Character defines your limits, but ambition is what pushes them.

CHAPTER 3: AMBITION

"Greed is a word weak men use to describe ambitious men."

Ambition is about how badly you want something. Think of someone holding your head underwater. How hard would you fight to come up for air? That same energy is what ambition feels like. You already know your "why". Ambition is the "how". It is how you move toward your goals, how you stay focused when things get tough, and how you build the life you want.

When I first joined the Army, my ambition was often misunderstood. I remember being told that whoever had the highest PT score would receive a waiver for promotion. That was all I needed to hear. We did physical training every morning, but every night I went on an extra run. I was determined to become the best version of myself.

The day came to take the test, and I finished my two-mile run in twelve minutes and fifty-one seconds, which remains my fastest run time in the Army. I was proud of that moment because my hard work had paid off. But as soon as I crossed the line, I felt a shift. Some people clapped and congratulated me, but others looked at me with jealousy. They did not see the extra hours of running or the nights I sacrificed to prepare. They only saw the result.

Not long after, I got promoted. The same people who had doubted me began calling me arrogant. That experience taught me something that has stayed with me ever since: people will always find a way to label ambition when they do not understand it. The real ones saw that I had a goal and went after it. The rest were lost in their own pride and personal failures.

That is what happens when your ambition begins to show. It makes people uncomfortable. It reveals who is truly for you and who is waiting for you to fail. But you cannot live for the opinions of others. Ambition is not for them. It is for you.

Ambition grows out of your "why". It is your way of fighting for air, your way of pushing forward. You already know you need to breathe. Ambition is what gets you up, keeps you going, and helps you rise after every setback.

Ambition and discipline go hand in hand. Discipline keeps you consistent, but ambition gives you the reason to keep showing up. I once heard someone say, "Do not let a crackhead out-hustle you." It sounds wild, but it is true. When there is a will, there is a way. Ambition is that will. It is what separates the talkers from the doers.

Sometimes people confuse ambition with greed. The difference is simple. Ambition is about bettering yourself and helping others along the way. Greed is about taking without giving. Ambition builds people up. Greed steps on others to get ahead.

Ambition grows with you. When you accomplish something, it gives you the confidence to do more. You begin to understand that success is not luck; it is the result of hard work and consistency. Ambition teaches you that you are capable of more than you ever thought possible.

But you also have to keep ambition in balance. There is a

difference between chasing goals and burning out. Being driven does not mean consistently running yourself into the ground. True ambition is patient. It understands that timing matters just as much as effort. You can be hungry without being reckless.

If a young person told me they are not sure what they are passionate about yet, I would tell them to start small. Passion is built through curiosity and commitment. Try different things until something sticks. The key is to never stop trying. The moment you give up on trying is the moment your ambition starts to die.

Every successful person you will ever meet built their ambition through small habits. Planning, preparation, prayer, and reflection are the things that feed ambition. You cannot just want success; you have to prepare for it. Write down your goals, track your progress, and learn from your mistakes. The more you plan, the more your ambition stays alive.

Ambition also requires humility. You cannot be too proud to learn from others. Some of the greatest lessons you will ever receive come from people who have already walked the path you are trying to take. Being ambitious without being coachable is like running hard in the wrong direction. Listen, learn, and adjust.

Ambition is a gift, but it is also a responsibility. Use it to lead by example. Use it to inspire others. When people see you move with purpose, it gives them permission to do the same. That is how ambition becomes contagious.

Remember, ambition will always test your patience and focus. You will face moments when no one believes in you. That is fine. Keep working. Let your results speak for you. Ambition is not about proving others wrong. It is about proving yourself right.

Reflection Questions:
- What goals make you feel truly alive when you think about them?
- Do you ever confuse ambition with greed or arrogance?
- How do you respond when someone misunderstands your ambition?
- How badly do you want to succeed, and what are you willing to do for it morally?

Ambition gets you started, but being willing to learn keeps you growing. Success is not just about how fast you move. It is about how much you are willing to absorb along the way.

CHAPTER 4: WILLING TO LEARN / LISTEN

"Real bosses do not talk, we just sit back and listen." – Dolph

One of the biggest lessons you can ever learn is that you do not know everything. Growth starts with humility and a willingness to learn and listen, even when the insight comes from people you least expect.

When I first arrived at my unit after basic training and initial training, I met another Soldier named McDonald. We called him Mac. He was a few years older than me, early twenties maybe, but he carried himself like someone who understood how to navigate the world. He had been around just long enough to know how things worked.

One Friday, Mac came up to me and said, "Hey, can you help me sweep and mop? I'm trying to leave early." At first, I did not question it. I just got up and helped. That moment turned into a life lesson I will never forget.

As we started cleaning, Mac told me he had already asked three other Soldiers to help, but they all looked at him like he was crazy. He laughed and said, "Dog, I just want to go home early, and I know leadership is going to tell us to clean up. I do not need someone to tell me to do what I already know needs to be done. Let's just knock it out now." We finished cleaning while the others stood around talking.

Sure enough, after we wrapped up, Mac walked straight to our Sergeant, explained what we had done, and asked if we could head out. The Sergeant smiled and said, "Mac, this is why I can count on you. You two go home. Enjoy the weekend." That was it. A simple lesson that stuck with me forever.

Mac was what we called a "high-speed" Soldier, sharp, dependable, and always two steps ahead. I learned from watching him. He did not wait for orders to do the right thing. He took initiative. When he got promoted later on, I felt proud, like I had a front-row seat to see the future of what good leadership looks like.

Before our deployment to Iraq, I was moved to another unit. That's when it hit me. I had become Mac. I took initiative, stayed one step ahead, and led by example. All because one person took the time to show me what right looked like. That small moment shaped the kind of person I became.

Being willing to learn and listen will take you further than talent ever will. You can have all the skill in the world, but if you are not coachable, you will eventually hit a wall. To be coachable means being able to listen, handle criticism, and make on-the-fly adjustments. You may not always like how the message is delivered, but that does not change the message. The truth remains the truth.

You have to maintain the confidence of knowing you are not perfect. There will never be a limit to excellence. No matter how good you are, there is always room to grow.

You can always tell who is uncoachable. It shows in their body language: the eye rolls, the sighs, the sucking of teeth.

They are already checked out. You do not even have to hear them speak because their attitude says it all. When they fail, they blame everyone else but themselves.

If I take the time to sit you down and explain what you need to fix, but you go out there and do the complete opposite, that is on you. I cannot help someone who refuses to help themselves. At that point, you belong to the streets.

Learning to take constructive criticism is key. Not everyone is out to attack you. Sometimes people are trying to sharpen you. Do not rely solely on your own understanding, as it will cost you more than you realize. Proverbs 3:5 speaks to this truth.

Listening is not a sign of weakness. It is a sign of wisdom. Some of the strongest leaders I have ever known are the ones who listen more than they speak. They absorb information, process it, and respond with purpose. You can learn from everyone and everything.

For young people, listening can be hard. You feel like you have something to prove. You want to show that you already know. But being teachable will put you ahead faster than pretending to have all the answers. Everyone loves confidence, but no one respects arrogance.

Here are a few ways to practice learning and listening:

1. Ask questions: Curiosity is the gateway to growth
2. Take notes: Write things down so they stick with you
3. Apply what you learn: Even small adjustments matter
4. Reflect: Ask yourself what you learned from each day
5. Stay humble: The goal is progress, not perfection

When you choose to listen, you gain something that no one can take away: experience. Experience builds judgment, and judgment builds wisdom. Wisdom allows you to see a situation clearly before it unfolds.

Listening is a skill that shapes your character. When you slow down long enough to hear people, you understand them better, respond better, and make better decisions. That is how you avoid mistakes and build stronger relationships.

Be willing to learn from anyone. Even a broken clock is right twice a day. Be humble enough to accept advice, even from those younger or less experienced than you. The key is being open enough to receive them.

Reflection Questions:
- Do you find it easy or hard to take advice from others? Why?
- Who in your life gives you honest feedback, and do you listen to them?
- What is one lesson you learned the hard way that you could have avoided by listening?
- How can you stay coachable as you become more successful?

Listening teaches you what to hear. Observation teaches you what to see. The more you pay attention, the more life reveals to you.

CHAPTER 5: LEARN THROUGH OBSERVATION

"Smart people learn from their mistakes. Wise people learn from the mistakes of others."

One of the best ways to grow in life is to simply pay attention. You do not have to touch every fire to know it burns. Being observant can be one of the most underrated skills a person can have. It teaches patience, awareness, and self-control. When you learn to watch how things play out, you gain wisdom without having to pay the same price someone else did.

I can think back to watching a close friend make all the wrong decisions. It was like watching an alternate version of myself. We came from the same background, had the same education, and shared the same opportunities. But he chose a different path. We stayed close, but some of the things he did were just downright confusing. It was like watching a train you knew was going to crash but being unable to stop it. I watched the consequences catch up to him. To this day, every time we talk, I think to myself, that could have been me.

If I had been around some of the same people he surrounded himself with, my story might have ended differently. But life has a way of whispering before it shouts. Just like earlier in my life, there were moments when I was told to "sit this one out." Looking back, I realize those moments were blessings. I am grateful that I learned through observation and not through reality.

You can learn a lot just by watching how people handle stress, how they treat others, and how they respond when things go wrong. The world is full of examples, both good and bad. All you have to do is pay attention.

Observation builds understanding. It teaches you that not everything requires your reaction. Some situations only require your attention. When you learn to slow down and watch, you start noticing the small details, like the tone of someone's voice, the shift in a room's energy, or the pattern of people's choices. That awareness becomes one of your greatest strengths.

I think some teens struggle with this because they feel like they have to experience everything firsthand. Some people just have to find out the hard way. I get it, we all learn differently. Some through reading, some through teaching, and others through hands-on experience. Life will teach you one way or another. If you are not willing to watch and listen, life becomes the teacher that charges the highest price.

If only more people would stop and look around, they would realize that the world is already showing them everything they need to see. Life is constantly giving hints. It is up to you to catch them.

Being observant also builds emotional intelligence. When you pay attention to the people around you, you begin to understand emotions, motives, and behaviors. You learn when to speak and when to stay quiet. You recognize when someone is hurting, when someone is lying, or when something just does not feel right. Observation keeps you sharp and aware.

I have seen people talk themselves out of opportunities simply because they were not paying attention. They miss the cues for when to listen, when to step up, and when to walk away. Sometimes silence is not weakness; it is wisdom. When you are observing, you are collecting information that others overlook. That information helps you move smarter.

For me, observation has always been a quiet superpower. I like being a fly on the wall, just watching and learning. You can learn how leaders lead, how people follow, and how emotions drive decisions. You can even learn who your real friends are. Just sit back, watch, and take mental notes. The world will show you more than you expect.

If you want to practice learning through observation, here are a few things that can help:
1) Stay alert: Pay attention to what is going on around you, not just what directly involves you.
2) Listen before you speak: The more you listen, the more you learn.
3) Reflect after experiences: Ask yourself what went right, what went wrong, and what you can take from it.
4) Watch patterns: When people or situations keep repeating themselves, there is always a lesson behind it.
5) Control your reactions: You cannot observe clearly when you are too emotional or defensive.

When you start practicing these habits, you realize how much life is teaching you every day. Every conversation, every mistake, every success, it is all a lesson waiting to be seen.

You learn from lessons, but distractions will always test your focus. The key difference is that a lesson builds you, while a distraction breaks your attention. If you ever catch yourself constantly asking, "How did I overlook that?" you probably got distracted. That is life's way of telling you to slow down and observe more closely.

Observation also connects directly to growth. The people who move the farthest in life are not always the loudest; they are the most aware. They notice the small things that others miss. They pay attention to their surroundings and understand situations before they unfold. Awareness is what keeps you sharp.

You do not need rank, age, or a title to lead. Sometimes the quietest person in the room is the one who sees the most. Observation gives you clarity, and clarity gives you power.

Keep your eyes open, your ears sharp, and your mind calm. The answers to most of your problems are already around you, you just have to pay attention long enough to see them.

Reflection Questions:
- What is one thing you learned just by watching someone else?
- How often do you slow down long enough to observe before reacting?
- Who in your life can you learn from right now without them even realizing it?
- How can you use what you observe to make better decisions?

Watching others teaches you what to do. Failing yourself teaches you how to grow. Observation is learning from the outside, but failure is learning from within.

CHAPTER 6: DON'T BE SCARED TO FAIL

"Failing is an event. Failure is a state of mind."

Failure is a part of life. It is guaranteed that you will fail at something. No matter how much you prepare, plan, or pray, it will happen. And when it does, it hurts. It messes with your confidence. It makes you question yourself: "Maybe I am not as good as I thought," or "Maybe I am not built for this." It happens to all of us. Failure is not the end. It is a checkpoint. It is how you grow.

There I was, around twenty-one, newly promoted to Sergeant at a new duty station. This was the first time I witnessed the consequences of failure and when I felt like I failed as a leader. My first Soldier, roughly nineteen, had just been assigned to me out of nowhere. He was newly married, had a baby, and was clearly overweight. At first, I did not think much of it. We all have room for improvement, and I figured a little discipline and teamwork could fix that.

Then came height and weight testing. He failed.

I made it my mission to help him. We did physical training together in the mornings, and I stayed late after work to run extra miles with him. I was putting in everything I had to help this Soldier succeed with five and six-mile runs, strength training, even encouraging him to eat better. But week after week, nothing changed.

Eventually, my leadership pulled me aside. "If he does not make progress," they said, "we are going to have to separate him from the Army."

I remember thinking: not my Soldier. I refused to believe he was going to give up like that.

One day, I skipped lunch to catch up on some paperwork. He came into the office with his lunch, sat down, and opened his food. Three slices of pizza, wings, Skittles, and a diet soda. My heart dropped. I was in disbelief. I sat there and realized something: I was doing everything I could, but he was not. I wanted to believe in him, but he did not believe in himself.

When it came time to separate him from the Army, I felt awkward. I kept thinking, Did I fail him as a leader? Deep down I knew he failed himself. There are consequences for every choice. His career, his family, and his stability were all on the line, and he chose to throw it away.

I got a call from his father, who happened to be a First Sergeant at another base. He wanted to know why I was kicking his son out. I told him the truth: "Your son is overweight, knows he is overweight, but chooses to eat poorly."

His father paused for a second and said, "Thank you. My son never fully explained."

The Soldier from my story did not fail because he was overweight; he failed because he gave up. He stopped trying. I failed as a leader as I should have caught his eating habits earlier.

Fail, but fall while still fighting.

If you can walk away from a failure saying, "I could have handled that differently," then you did not lose, you learned. You took something from the experience that will make you stronger next time. The only real failure is quitting.

People give up too easy. The moment something goes wrong, they fold. But growth only comes through friction. Diamonds are formed under pressure.

You will fail at something eventually. You will stumble. You will doubt yourself. But every single failure comes with an opportunity to rise.

When I think about failure now, I do not see it as the end of the road. I see it as a redirection. Every "no" I have ever received was just pointing me toward a better "yes." Every setback pushed me to work harder, think smarter, and stay disciplined.

The people who bounce back from failure do one thing differently, they accept responsibility. They do not make excuses. They accept what happened, learn from it, and move forward. Accountability turns failure into fuel.

If a young person came to me and said, "I'm scared to try because I don't want to fail," I would tell them this, you will never know if you never go for it. I would rather fail chasing something than stay stagnant doing nothing. You cannot learn from a path you never walked.

Failure is not the opposite of success. It is part of success. Every lesson you learn through failure puts you one step closer to mastering your craft. Each setback refines you, humbles you, and prepares you for your next opportunity.

Do not be scared to fail. Be scared to quit.

Day One>One Day

Every failure you survive makes you stronger. Every mistake you reflect on makes you wiser.

Every fall you recover from makes you tougher.

If you ever start to doubt yourself, remember this, you are not starting over. You are starting smarter.

Failing is an event. Failure is a state of mind. Keep moving. Keep learning. Keep fighting. Because the only true failure is when you stop trying.

Reflection Questions:
- When was the last time you failed, and what did it teach you?
- Do you focus more on what went wrong or what you learned?
- How do you usually respond when something does not go as planned?
- What does "bouncing back" look like for you right now?

Failure shows you what went wrong. Discipline ensures it does not happen again. The real test is not whether you fall, it is whether you have the strength to get back up and keep moving.

CHAPTER 7: DISCIPLINE

"Discipline is doing what you have to do, even when you do not want to do it."

Discipline is not fun, and it is rarely exciting. It is the quiet work that no one sees. It is the habits, routines, and commitments that separate those who wish from those who win.

Motivation gets you started, but discipline keeps you going.

I still remember prepping to attend the Warrior Leaders Course (WLC). It is a leadership course in the Army designed to test your physical, mental, and leadership abilities. I knew I was not the best runner, but I also knew there was no way I was going there unprepared. At the time, I was running my two-mile in about fourteen and a half minutes. Decent, but not great. My goal was to hit thirteen minutes flat. I did not know what the course route would look like or what the terrain would be, but I made up my mind that I would be ready no matter what.

Every morning, I ran. Then I started running again at night. It did not matter if it was cold, raining, or if I had a long day. I ran anyway. While others relaxed after work, I laced up my shoes and hit the pavement. It is funny how no one pays attention when you are being still, but the moment you start moving with purpose, everyone suddenly wants your time. My friends would hit me up with the same lines: "Let's go out!" or "Let's chill." My response was always the same: No, I am training.

I wanted to do well, not for attention, not for bragging rights, but because I had made a commitment to myself. When I got to WLC, all that work paid off. I ran thirteen minutes and fifteen second two-mile and crushed the other events. That feeling was everything, not because it came easy, but because I had earned it.

The side effect of that discipline was even better. After WLC, I was so used to working out after work that I just kept doing it. Running turned into gym sessions. It became part of who I am today. What started as preparation became a lifestyle. That is the power of discipline: it turns effort into identity.

Most people struggle with discipline because they rely too much on motivation. Motivation feels good, but it fades fast. Discipline is the engine that keeps you moving when motivation is gone.

Motivation might get you out of bed once. Discipline will keep you getting up early every day. Motivation might help you start a diet. Discipline will keep you eating clean after everyone else quits. Motivation is temporary. Discipline is permanent.

The problem is that people want quick results. They go hard for a few weeks, lose a few pounds, get some compliments, and then stop. They think the job is done. But discipline does not have a finish line. You do not just "arrive" one day and stop trying.

Discipline is a lifelong process.

To maintain discipline, you have to know your "why." Your "why" gives discipline meaning. Without it, you will always burn out. When you know why you are doing something, even the hard days make sense. The reason matters more than the reward.

When you are disciplined, you learn that consistency is the secret to everything. It is the only answer that truly works. You can talk about goals all you want, but without discipline, they are just wishes.

If you want to build discipline, start with something simple. Read a book every month. Go to the gym three times a week. Wake up fifteen minutes earlier. Pray or meditate daily. Discipline is not built in grand gestures; it is built in small, repeated actions that create results over time.

You do not need to overhaul your life. You just need to start somewhere and stay consistent.

Discipline is not limited to physical training. It applies to every part of life—your finances, relationships, career, and faith. Discipline is saying no to things that bring short-term pleasure so you can have long-term peace. It is choosing to save instead of spend. It is controlling your emotions instead of reacting out of anger. It is staying loyal when it would be easier to walk away.

When you live with discipline, you develop control. Not control over others, but control over yourself. And that is the highest form of power.

If I could give advice to a young person about discipline, I would tell them to stop waiting for the perfect moment. It will never come. There will always be a reason to skip today, to put it off until tomorrow. The only perfect time to start is now.

Discipline is like a muscle. The more you use it, the stronger it gets. The less you use it, the weaker it becomes.

Discipline is not built in the spotlight. It is built in the shadows—when no one is cheering you on, when you are tired, when you could quit but choose not to. Those moments define you.

At some point, you will have to choose between your feelings and your future. Discipline is choosing your future every single time.

When I look back at all the progress I have made, it was never because of motivation. It was because of discipline. The decision to stay consistent, to show up when I did not feel like it, and to keep pushing forward. Discipline is what separates the dreamers from the doers. It is the quiet voice that says, "Keep going."

Reflection Questions:
- What is one area of your life that would improve with more discipline?
- How do you keep going when you are not motivated?
- Do you see discipline as punishment or as preparation?
- What is one routine you can start today that your future self will thank you for?

Discipline builds habits, but your circle reinforces them. The people around you will either feed your discipline or destroy it. Choose your company wisely.

CHAPTER 8: GUILTY BY ASSOCIATION

"Not only are you responsible for the energy you bring, but
you're also responsible for the energy you surround yourself
with." — Oprah Winfrey

Guilty by association is a real thing. I never understood it
when I was younger. It took growing up to realize how my
circle of friends all ended up doing the same things. In math,
you learn to recognize patterns. It is hard to say you are an
even number when you have odd behavior.

The people you spend time with influence you more than you
think. Even when you believe you are your own person, their
habits, words, and mindset start to shape you. Over time, you
begin to mirror the energy around you. That is why it is
important to question your personal reasons for being friends
with someone.

"Why am I close to this person?"

"What do they bring into my life?"

Sometimes, we may find out that we are the negative one in
the group. Other times, we discover that the people closest to
us have been quietly hoping we fail.

Jealousy is sneaky. It has no boundaries. It can come from a
parent, a sibling, a coworker, or a friend. You never really
know who wants to see you do well and who is secretly

hoping you do not. That is why I prefer to know my enemies upfront. There is no guesswork. If it is "forget me," then it is "forget you" too. It is that simple.

Surround yourself with people who align with your goals. For me, that means people who value God, family, self-development, finances, and hobbies. My circle reflects those same priorities.

When I joined the Army, I met a guy named Wright. He is still one of my best friends to this day. We went through basic training together and pushed each other every step of the way throughout our careers. If I learned something, I would share it with him, and he did the same for me. There was a friendly sense of competition between us, we both wanted to see each other win. That is what real friendship looks like: not jealousy, not comparison, just two people holding each other accountable and growing together. Wright's presence taught me that the right circle does not drain you, it fuels you. They remind you of what you are capable of, even when you forget.

You can tell when someone genuinely wants the best for you. They rarely bring up dark times or past mistakes. They understand what you are going through and want to see you come out better on the other side.

Be cautious of fake friends. Some people only show up when it benefits them. As you grow older, especially in your late teens and early twenties, your circle will change, and that is normal.

Think about high school. Some people were only successful because of their parents. Their routines were managed for them—waking up early, doing homework, maintaining appearances. But once the structure of school and parental control faded, you start to see who really has discipline and drive and who was just going through the motions.

Never feel guilty when this happens. Understand that some people mature, and some do not. Growth can be lonely, but it is necessary. You can love people from a distance without losing your peace.

You will know when you are surrounded by the right people. Their goals will mirror your own. They will challenge you to keep up, not hold you back. I always look for long-term vision, consistency, and self-development in the people around me.

If someone is still dealing with the same problems they had three years ago and has made no effort to change, it might be time to separate yourself. Growth means moving forward. When your old crowd says, "You changed," that is your confirmation that you are doing something right. Of course, you changed. Between eighteen and twenty-four, life hits fast with college, relationships, family, and finances—everything shifts. The real question is, why haven't they?

You can also tell a lot about someone by how they treat others. Watch how people act toward waiters, bank tellers, or cashiers. If someone is rude to people who cannot do anything for them, that is all you need to know. That is not my type of person.

The same goes for gossip. I cannot stand people who always have a negative story. You mean to tell me the most exciting thing that happened in your day was that Brenda lost her job or that Starbucks messed up your drink order? Keep that energy away from me.

If you are non-confrontational, I understand that cutting people off can be hard. But sometimes, you have to. If you keep negative people around you long enough, you start to sound like them. Their problems become your mindset. That energy rubs off, and before you know it, you are carrying weight that is not even yours.

A good circle will make you want to do better. Even if you are the procrastination type, that energy will rub off on you. A good friend will see you slipping and pull you back on track. That is the kind of friendship you need.

You know you have a solid circle when you can admit that you failed at something and instead of laughing, they help you find a way forward. If you tell them you failed a class, they say, "Why didn't you tell me you were struggling? Here's what helped me." That is love. That is accountability.

Growing out of friendships is hard, but it happens. After high school, most people start going their separate ways. It is not always personal; life just changes. The structure that used to keep you connected, like school and daily routines, disappears. That is when you start to see people for who they really are.

Sometimes that realization hurts. You realize you were holding on to a memory of who someone used to be, not who they actually are now. But that is part of growth. Everyone is not meant to go where you are going.

When it comes to your circle, pay attention to patterns. Watch who shows up when you are doing well and who disappears when you are struggling. Watch who claps for you when you succeed and who changes the subject when you shine.

I once heard, "You become the sum of the five people you spend the most time with." If you surround yourself with people who complain, you will find something to complain about too. But if you surround yourself with people who push, plan, and execute, that becomes your standard.

Your circle will either sharpen you or dull you.

Choose wisely.

Reflection Questions:
- Do your friends push you forward or hold you back?
- Who in your circle motivates you to be better?
- Have you ever outgrown a friendship that no longer fit your goals?
- What does a healthy circle look like to you right now?

Once you know who belongs in your circle, the next step is learning how to move within it, when to speak, when to listen, and when to simply read the room.

CHAPTER 9: READ THE ROOM

"Be the thermostat, not the thermometer. Control the energy, don't just react to it."

Reading the room is one of the most important life skills you can learn. It is about being socially aware of everything around you. It is not about shrinking yourself or pretending to be something you are not. It is about knowing when to speak, when to listen, and when to simply observe.

I always use this analogy: be the thermostat, not the thermometer. A thermometer only reacts to temperature, but a thermostat sets it. You can turn the heat up and energize everyone or turn it down to calm a situation. That is what social awareness is. You know and feel what you are walking into.

Even in small situations, reading the room matters. If I hear someone gossip in church, I am done talking to them. You are too immature for me. If we are in a conversation and kids are close by, but you keep cursing like nothing changed, you are showing me that you do not understand timing or respect. Read the room.

There is a time and place for everything. If you are hanging out with your friends, sure, laugh and be loose. But if you are talking to elders, teachers, or mentors, your attitude and presence should adjust. It does not mean you are fake.

It means you understand where you are and how to carry yourself in that space.

I like to keep it simple: I would never take my grandma to a strip club with me. That does not mean I am two different people. It just means I have common sense.

You will see plenty of people fail to read the room and say, "That is just how I am." That line alone tells you everything you need to know. I have seen people ruin job interviews because they started cursing. I have seen a guy talk trash to a professional fighter. We all saw the cauliflower ear, but he missed the cue. He paid for it.

Even in friendships, timing matters. If your friend just told you their parent passed, that is not the time to ask everyone what they are planning for Father's Day. Read the room.

Paying attention can save your life. Understanding the climate in a room is a skill. If I walk into a space and see tension, let's say some guys are arguing, I immediately look for the exits. I am not leaving yet, but I know where I need to go if things get worse.

Awareness can keep you alert.

Stay alert.

Stay alive.

On the other hand, if I see someone is depressed or withdrawn, I can try to build them up. But I also know when to step away. Some situations drain you if you stay too long, even when your heart is in the right place. That too, is part of reading the room.

Experience teaches you when to adjust. You do not wake up one day and magically know what to do. You learn from the moments when you got it wrong. You learn from watching others and paying attention to how different people react.

No one teaches us how to pick up social cues, but over time, you start to feel energy shift. You can tell when something is off just by body language, such as crossed arms, a forced smile, people checking their phones, or broken eye contact. That is your sign to adjust.

I have been in rooms where I felt like I did not belong, and instead of talking more, I watched. That is where I learned the most. Reading the room is not just about talking less; it is about observing and understanding what is happening before you react.

Stay yourself, but be smart. If you cannot tell your parents the exact details of where you are, what you are doing, or what was said, it is probably inappropriate. Pay attention to how people are presenting themselves. If you walk into a room and everyone is dressed professionally, sitting with notebooks and pens out, you should probably do the same. That is your cue. You did not do your homework if you show up underdressed or unprepared.

Scanning a room should become second nature. Look for engagement. Are people paying attention, laughing, bored, or uncomfortable? That tells you how to adjust your tone, attitude, or delivery.

If you ever find yourself in a professional setting where

someone starts using profanity or bringing the wrong energy, that is your sign to keep your composure and let them disqualify themselves. Do not follow their lead. You are there for a reason. Reading the room is about awareness, control, and respect. It means knowing what is happening around you, being able to adjust your energy, and understanding boundaries. Every space has a purpose. Some are meant for laughter, others for learning, and others for listening.

When you can do all of that, people notice. They see you as mature, dependable, and confident. Those are the traits that open doors.

Reading the room is not about pretending. It is about protecting your image, your opportunities, and your peace. The person who can adapt without changing who they are will always win.

Reflection Questions:
- How often do you stop to notice what is happening around you before speaking or acting?
- Can you tell when the mood of a room shifts?
- Have you ever misread a situation and learned from it?
- What can you do to become more socially aware in everyday life?

Once you can read the room, the next step is learning how to understand the people in it because awareness means nothing if you do not know who you are speaking to.

CHAPTER 10: KNOWING YOUR AUDIENCE

"Never be limited by other people's limited imaginations."
Dr. Mae Jemison

Knowing your audience is another underrated skill you should learn and develop. It is the ability to read a situation, understand who you are speaking to, and adjust how you deliver your message without losing who you are. This is effective and a smart choice you can make in life.

You do not talk to your parents the same way you talk to your friends, right? You already know your audience. You understand that there is a time and place for certain things, and there are lines that should not be crossed. That simple awareness is emotional intelligence and a major key to success.

Let's be real. There are things you would never do in front of your parents or grandparents. You would not curse, play certain songs, or tell wild stories about your weekend. You would not walk into the house using slang or inside jokes your friends would understand but your parents would not. It is not because you are scared of them; it is because you respect them and the environment you are in.

That same level of awareness applies everywhere. The way you speak to your coach, teacher, or boss will always look different from the way you talk to your best friend. It is not about changing your personality. It is about knowing when to shift gears. If you know how to read people and respond the right way, you can go far.

Knowing your audience is the difference between being understood and being misunderstood. The person who cannot adapt often ends up frustrated, saying things like, "People just don't get me." No, they hear you fine; you just did not deliver your message in a way they could receive it.

I once told someone that I went from saying, "You got me messed up," to, "Let's revisit our expectations of one another." That right there is knowing your audience. It is not that you changed; it is that you learned when to use your words wisely.

People who say, "This is just how I am," often limit themselves. They use that line to excuse behavior that holds them back. Real confidence means you can walk into any room—classroom, interview, meeting, or conversation with your parents—and still be yourself while also being aware of your surroundings.

You can be authentic and adaptable at the same time. The two are not opposites.

When you learn to know your audience, you gain control over how you are perceived. You can take the same story, the same message, and deliver it in ten different ways depending on who you are talking to. That skill alone will open more doors than any GPA or test score ever could.

For example, let's say you just got your first paycheck, and you are proud of it. If you talk to your friends, you might celebrate and joke about it. If you talk to your parents, you might focus on the responsibility that comes with earning money. The message is the same "I'm proud of my progress" but the delivery changes based on your audience.

This skill can save you from unnecessary conflict. If someone is upset, that is not the time to make a joke. If someone is venting, that is the time to listen, not interrupt. When you understand what the other person needs in the moment, you respond with awareness, not emotion.

If you notice that no matter what you say, the person is not listening, hear me out: that is a sign they are not your audience. Walk away. Not every conversation is worth your energy. Sometimes the best way to be heard is to stop talking.

Knowing your audience also applies to your digital presence. The internet is one big room, and everyone in it is watching. Before you post, ask yourself, "Who is going to see this, and what message am I sending?" What might be funny to your friends could look reckless to your boss or future college. Be intentional. Represent yourself in a way that future you will be proud of.

You do not need to share every opinion or every moment online. Some things are better lived than posted. The ability to control what you share and how you share it is part of maturity.

When you master the skill of knowing your audience, you are developing something even greater: emotional intelligence. You learn when to speak, when to listen, and when to adjust. You understand that success often depends on how you connect with people. You will find that the person who listens and adapts usually goes further than the one who insists on always being right.

So, before you walk into any room, classroom, or conversation, pause for a moment and ask yourself "Who am I talking to" followed by "How do I want them to remember me?"

Those two questions can change everything.

Reflection Questions:
- How does the way you communicate change depending on who you are talking to?
- Have you ever said the right thing at the wrong time? What did you learn from it?
- How do you balance being authentic while staying respectful to your environment?
- When was the last time listening helped you understand someone better?

Once you understand how to communicate with your audience, the next step is making sure what they see matches who you are. That is where appearance comes in because presentation speaks before your words ever do.

CHAPTER 11: APPEARANCE

"Dress how you want to be addressed."

Appearance is extremely important. It is the first impression, and a lot of people get it wrong. Your appearance is not just what you wear. It is your grooming, your attitude, your posture, and your presence. It is how you carry yourself before you ever say a word.

Imagine someone vouching for you and setting up an opportunity, but you show up looking like you just rolled out of bed. That person's reputation is now tied to your lack of effort. Your appearance is a reflection of respect, not only for yourself but also for the people who put their name on the line for you.

To put this into perspective, think about a restaurant. A good friend tells you they have the best food in town, so you decide to check it out. You are excited, expecting a great experience. You pull up, but the first thing you see is broken blinds, a crooked sign, and a cardboard box filling in for a window. The parking lot looks a little sketchy, but you try to look past it. You tell yourself, "The food must be worth it."

Still trying to give it a fair chance, you walk in and immediately notice a smell. Not the smell of good food, but the faint, stale odor of carpet that should have been replaced years ago. They have a plant wall, but it is dusty. You look around and see tables that have not been wiped down, sticky floors, and plastic cups. The hostess barely looks up, clearly annoyed that you walked in. You finally get seated, and you are still trying to be patient.

You ask for sweet tea, and they say they are out. You ask for a soda, and the machine is down. You ask for water, and they have that. When the waitress brings it out, you touch the cup and it is greasy. You are done. At that point, it does not matter how good the food might be. You are leaving.

That restaurant is you.

You might have the best personality, the strongest work ethic, or the kindest heart, but if your presentation is sloppy, people will never stick around long enough to find out. When you walk into a room, people are analyzing quickly, not because they enjoy judging, but because we all look for signs. Just like that restaurant, your appearance sets the tone for what people expect from you.

Your clothes do not have to be expensive, but they should be clean and fit well. If your shirt has a stain on it, it sends a message that you did not care enough to prepare. If your shoes are scuffed and dirty, it looks like you rush through life without paying attention to detail. If your hands are dry, your nails dirty, or your breath is bad, that says more about your priorities than your words ever will.

Appearance is not about vanity. It is about pride. The little things speak louder than you think. People will notice if your collar is wrinkled, if your teeth look unbrushed, or if you look like you rolled out of bed and showed up because you had to. The same way you would never return to that dirty restaurant, people will not come back to someone who looks like they do not care.

Think about it. Would you feel confident eating at a restaurant that looked unclean, no matter how good the reviews are? Probably not. So why should someone trust you with opportunity, responsibility, or leadership if you look unprepared?

That restaurant had all the potential in the world, but its lack of care ruined the experience. The same applies to people.

If you do not value your appearance, why should anyone else? When you show up looking disorganized, people may assume that is how you approach life too. You only get one chance to make a first impression, and those few seconds can change everything about how people treat you.

I think ironing has become a lost art. People rely on the excuse that "looks should not matter," but they do. You do not have to be rich or flashy. Just put care into your presentation. Walk with confidence. Keep your head up and your attitude sharp. People notice.

When I see someone who is put together, it stands out. It does not mean they are perfect, it means they took the time to prepare. That small act speaks volumes about character and self-respect.

When I hear people say "accept me as I am," I understand what they mean, but I also think they forget that it works both ways. You can want people to accept you for who you are, but that does not mean they have to. In professional settings especially, appearance is not just self-expression, it is a standard.

If you are applying for a job, meeting someone's parents, or stepping into an important event, presentation matters. Showing up unprepared or looking careless tells people that you do not take the opportunity seriously. You cannot get upset when people react accordingly.

People will judge before you speak, not because they are cruel, but because that is how perception works. The goal is not to please everyone, but to show that you respect yourself enough to put effort into how you show up. Even on your worst days, your posture and presence speak for you. Walk like you belong. Carry yourself with quiet confidence. There is no need to announce who you are when your energy already says it.

Appearance might not define your character, but it will open or close doors before people ever get the chance to know your character.

Taking care of yourself is not pride, it is discipline.

Reflection Questions:
- What does your appearance say about you before you speak?
- How much effort do you put into your personal presentation?
- Why do you think first impressions are so powerful?
- What small details could you improve to look more prepared and confident?

Once you master your appearance, the next step is how you carry it with your presence and confidence. Looking the part means nothing if you cannot stand tall and believe in the person behind the clothes.

CHAPTER 12: PRESENCE AND CONFIDENCE

"Confidence is silent. Insecurities are loud."

Presence is what and how you carry yourself. It is the combination of your character, your appearance, and your awareness of the space you are in. Presence and confidence go hand in hand.

Confidence is not arrogance. Confidence is knowing you have done the work and deserve to be in that room, at that table, or in that position. Arrogance is pretending you belong without putting in the effort to earn it. The biggest difference between the two is that confidence makes room for others, while arrogance only makes room for itself.

Confidence radiates. Think about the person giving a presentation who does not need to read from the slides. They know the material, they understand the topic, and they believe in what they are saying. That kind of energy fills a room. Confidence is not about being the loudest person there, it is about being the one people listen to when you finally speak.

Some people are born with presence. Maybe they were the oldest sibling and had to take charge early. Others develop it over time through experience and reflection.

Presence is the product of self-awareness, knowing when to

speak, when to listen, and when to just stand tall and let your energy speak for you.

I remember sitting in a classroom years ago, watching two students give presentations back to back. One read word for word from the screen, barely making eye contact. The other spoke from the heart, walked with purpose, and kept the audience engaged. Both had the same information, but only one had presence. It was not about popularity or looks, it was about the confidence built through preparation. That was when I learned that presence is built, not given.

Even the most confident people have moments of doubt. I have had times where I questioned if I was good enough or if I belonged in certain spaces. Over time, I learned that preparation builds confidence. When you know your material, know your role, and know your purpose, you stop worrying about what could go wrong and start focusing on making it right.

Confidence does not mean you have all the answers. It means you are comfortable enough with yourself to learn, adapt, and admit when you are wrong. Humility is confidence under control.

You can tell when someone lacks confidence, they overcompensate. They talk too much, try too hard, or act like they have it all figured out. Confidence is calm. It does not chase validation.

Sit up straight. Make eye contact. Offer a firm handshake. Speak clearly. Those small details matter. Body language is half the message you send, and people read it before they hear your words.

Preparation and self-discipline build confidence. When you put in the work, you stop hoping you belong and start knowing you do. It is like studying for a test. When you actually study, you walk in calm because you already know you can handle it.

True confidence starts with self-acceptance. You have to genuinely like who you are. You cannot fake confidence if you dislike yourself inside. When you love yourself, you carry a different kind of energy, one that says, "I know who I am, and I am okay with that."

It has to be in you, not on you.

Reflection Questions:
- How do you define confidence in your own words
- Have you ever struggled with self-doubt, and how did you overcome it
- What does your body language say about you in a room full of people
- How can you balance confidence with humility

Once you build presence and confidence, the next piece of success is knowing how to protect your peace. Because even strong, confident people burn out if they never slow down and recharge.

CHAPTER 13: PEACE AND BALANCE

"Even God rested on the seventh day."

After everything we have covered, I would be remiss to skip over the importance of peace and balance. Most parents will never tell you this because they want you to grind, grind, grind. But I will happily tell you it is okay to blow off some steam.

Go out, have some fun, make friends, celebrate your wins, splurge occasionally, hit the gym, sew that scarf, work on that project car, go to the club, or read a book. Whatever you need to do to relax, do it. Give your brain a breather. You deserve it.

Take time to drown out the noise. In today's world, it is easy to get lost in the pressure of always being productive and always striving for the next big thing. But balance is key. You cannot push forward all the time without burning out. And you should not feel guilty for taking a break because you cannot give your best if you are running on empty.

Find a hobby. That is something I feel most people no longer make time for, and instead, social media fills that void. Go sign up for a dance class if that is your thing. For me, I love the gym and running. Honestly, part of it is probably just an excuse to listen to music, but hey, that is me.

Having hobbies is healthy. It is about clearing your mind and finding an outlet where you can truly disconnect. A hobby, something that takes your full attention and brings you joy, can be the perfect way to reset. Even something simple like building a Lego set or putting a puzzle together can be therapeutic. That time spent focusing on something else heals you, refuels your energy, and keeps you sharp for the bigger goals ahead.

I think teens today struggle with finding peace because there is so much demand placed on them. We ask 17-year-olds to pick out a major and choose a career path, which basically means deciding what they are going to do for the rest of their lives. That is a lot of pressure, especially when you do not have everything figured out yet. Then, when they start heading in one direction, adults criticize them for being immature or too young to know better. It feels like no one is telling them that it is okay to have fun, to explore, and to mess up a little. You are still in the process of figuring things out. The constant weight of expectations can make it hard to focus on balance. But if you do not take care of your mind and your peace, everything else will fall apart.

Personally, I am all over the place when it comes to finding my peace. Growing up, weekends were tough for me. I dreaded it because I knew it meant one thing: cleaning day. My mom would throw on gospel music or R&B, and we would clean the entire house. I hated it at the time. But now, I see the value in that time.

Cleaning is important to me because it represents clearing the clutter, not just physically but mentally. A clean environment equals a clear mind. And when I take the time to clean, it feels like I am organizing my thoughts and prioritizing my peace. It is my way of resetting.

I also love to cook. Cooking is a vulnerable yet therapeutic experience for me. It is about showing gratitude to the people I am cooking for, putting love and care into every dish. There is nothing better than seeing someone enjoy something I personally made. That is peace too. It is about creating something meaningful and enjoying the process without rushing it.

I feel like everyone works out now, so it is almost cliché to mention it. Working out has a lot in common with life. Consistency is key. If you stay at it and you push yourself, you will see results. If you barely put in effort, you will get nothing in return. I love competing with myself. It is not about being better than anyone else. It is about becoming a better version of myself than I was yesterday.

Peace is not just about doing nothing. It is about balance. It is about knowing when to hustle and when to rest. Even God needed a day of rest. We forget that sometimes. We get caught in the whirlwind of life and think we need to go, go, go. But without balance, you burn out. Without peace, you lose focus.

It is easy to get caught up in the noise, to let pressure and expectations push you to keep striving, but you have to recognize the value of rest. Without rest, you will not have the energy or clarity to keep moving forward. Burnout is real, and it is something you can avoid if you take the time to prioritize your peace.

You cannot be productive all the time. You cannot chase success and ignore your mental health. It is not sustainable. Peace and balance are not luxuries, they are necessary. They are the foundation that allows you to handle life's chaos, maintain focus, and keep your energy high.

Even on your worst days, take a moment to rest. You need balance. Because when you are at peace with yourself, you can conquer anything life throws at you.

Reflection Questions:
- When was the last time you took time to truly rest?
- What hobbies or activities bring you peace?
- How do you handle stress when life feels overwhelming?
- Are you giving yourself permission to slow down and breathe?

Once you have mastered your appearance, presence, and balance, you are ready for the next challenge, building confidence and trusting that you are enough, no matter the journey ahead.

CHAPTER 14: TIME IS CURRENCY

"You can make more money, but you can't make more time."

Time is currency. It is another way of saying do not waste your time, do not waste your energy, do not waste your effort, and do not wait for anything. Once you start viewing your time the same way you view money, everything in your life changes.

You can spend time, you can save time, or you can waste time, but you can never get it back. Every second you give away to something unimportant is time stolen from something that could change your future.

We tend to get caught up in things that honestly do not matter. Drama seems to be the biggest one. Arguments, rumors, fake friendships, and people who constantly pull you into their problems. It is all unimportant. These are things you will forget in less than a year, yet they eat up hours of your energy today.

Relationships, whether romantic or friendly, are another time trap when you do not manage them well. If someone truly supports you, they will show it through their actions, not just their words. Be around people who value your time as much as their own. The wrong crowd will drain your energy faster than anything else.

Then there is procrastination, the silent thief. Everyone struggles with it at some point, but think about it like this. Imagine working hard for months to reach a goal, finally getting close, and then losing momentum because you simply do not feel like finishing. You have already done the hard part. You have invested your time, energy, and focus. Why stop now?

Procrastination is like paying rent on a house you never move into. You keep investing but never see the reward. Finish what you start. Do not let laziness turn your progress into regret.

Another major time killer is waiting. Waiting for the right moment, the perfect opportunity, or for someone else to make the first move. Waiting is dangerous because it feels harmless. You tell yourself you will start tomorrow or next week, but tomorrow turns into months and months turn into years.

If you are praying for something, pray with purpose. Do not pray and wait. Pray and move. Meet God halfway. Faith without effort is wishful thinking. I pray in a way that sounds like this: "Lord, I do not know what I am doing, but I pray I learn along the way, and it leads me to where you need me to be." Prayer gives direction, but movement creates progress.

I used to struggle with staying up late, my mind running in circles replaying everything from the day. Someone once told me to write everything down before bed, to get it out of my head and onto paper. It changed everything. My brain finally had permission to rest. That small change taught me something about time. Sometimes your peace of mind depends on how well you manage your hours. We all have the same 24 hours, but what you do with them separates progress from falling backwards.

Social media is one of the biggest distractions of our time. It can be a useful tool, but it can also be a black hole that drains hours before you realize it. You start scrolling for just a minute, and before you know it, an hour is gone. That hour could have gone toward your goals, your fitness, your relationships, or your personal growth.

Get off your phone. Go do something that feeds your mind or your body. Pick up a hobby that gives you real satisfaction, something that requires focus and creativity. Build something, fix something, learn something. Hobbies keep you grounded and give you a healthy way to recharge.

When you learn to manage your time, everything else starts to fall into place. You begin seeing life as a series of investments. Every action becomes a deposit or a withdrawal from your future.

Time circles back to your goals and your "why". When you understand what drives you, managing time becomes easier. Priorities shift every day, but your top goals, your reason for doing what you do, should always stay within your top five.

Time management is not about being busy all the time. It is about being intentional. Ask yourself daily, "Did what I do today get me closer to where I want to be?" If the answer is no, then you know what needs to change.

Every time you hit snooze, every time you delay an assignment, and every time you say you will do it later, you are making a withdrawal from your future.

When you spend time wisely, it compounds like interest. Small daily habits, like waking up early, studying an extra hour, or reading before bed, all add up. Time rewards those who respect it.

You cannot buy time back. You cannot refund wasted years or trade them in for better ones. You can only learn to treat your time as something sacred, something worth protecting.

Ask yourself this:

"Do you have a negative balance on your time?"

"Are you overspending on things that do not matter, or investing in what builds your future?"

Time is your most valuable currency. Spend it wisely.

Reflection Questions:
- How do you currently spend most of your time each day?
- What activities are draining your time without giving anything back?
- What would your schedule look like if you only focused on your goals?
- How can you start spending your time more intentionally?

Time is what connects your goals to your results. But while you are building your future, do not forget that what you do online can shape it too. Your next opportunity could depend on what your digital footprint says about you.

CHAPTER 15: DIGITAL FOOTPRINT

"The internet never forgets."

Your digital footprint is the trail you leave behind online. Every post, comment, picture, and like becomes part of your story, even when you think it is gone. What you post today might follow you for years, shaping how people see you long after you have changed.

To you, it might be a joke. To someone else, it is a statement about your character. The things you post might seem harmless in the moment, a funny video, a quick rant, or a meme that made you laugh, but screenshots last forever. Once it is out there, you lose control of how people interpret it. That is what most people miss. It is not just about what you post, it is about the overall perception.

Social media can be a great tool if you use it wisely. You can connect with people, build a network, or promote your talents and goals. But when you use it carelessly, it can limit your opportunities before you even know it. Employers, schools, and mentors all check social media now. It is one of the first places they look. They are not just reviewing your grades or your résumé, they are searching for clues about your judgment, maturity, and mindset. They want to see how you handle yourself when no one is watching. Can you represent their overall brand well?

You do not want your digital footprint to say that you are reckless, unprofessional, or negative. You want it to say that you are focused, disciplined, and aware.

If you would not say something out loud in front of your parents, teachers, or future employer, it probably does not belong online.

I once saw an NCO get in serious trouble for posting a video on TikTok. It started as something harmless, just a short clip of them dancing in uniform while on duty. The video went viral, but not for the right reasons. Leadership got involved, and what was meant to be funny turned into a formal counseling statement, written reports, and embarrassment that spread across the entire organization. The lesson was clear, the uniform, the environment, and the timing all matter. The internet does not care about your intentions, it only shows the results. That one moment followed them for months and reminded everyone watching that not every post is worth the risk.

Sometimes people think deleting a post means it is gone. It is not. Once something is shared, it can be saved, forwarded, or stored by anyone who sees it. A deleted post might disappear from your profile, but it can still live somewhere else. It can still live with someone else. That is the part no one tells you.

Think before you post. Ask yourself, "What story does this tell about me?" If the answer is one you would not want others to read, do not post it.

Your digital footprint is not just about what to avoid, it is also about what to build.

You can use your online presence to open doors, not close them. A football player can post highlights to get noticed by coaches. A student can share achievements and tag schools or scholarship programs. A creative person can post their art, music, or writing and build a platform. Social media is a tool. How you use it determines whether it works for you or against you.

You do not need a huge following to make an impact. You just need purpose. Use your digital space to represent your goals and the type of person you are striving to become.

When someone searches your name, what will they see? Will it reflect someone who takes pride in their growth, or someone still chasing attention? The internet gives you a voice, but it also gives you responsibility. Your words can travel further than you ever intended. A single post can inspire people or it can hurt them. You may not always realize how far your influence reaches, but once your words are out there, they belong to everyone who reads them. Use that power wisely. Use it to motivate, to uplift, or to share knowledge. Be intentional. Build a digital version of yourself that mirrors the person you want to be in real life.

If someone followed your account for a month, would they know your values? Would they see effort, purpose, and direction? Or would they see confusion, negativity, and drama?

Be the person who adds value, not noise.

We live in a world where attention is important. Everyone wants likes, views, and followers. None of that lasts. What lasts is reputation. Once it is damaged, it is hard to repair.

Do not let social media write a story that you cannot defend later. Every post, every comment, and every like leaves a mark. Build a trail that you can be proud of. Your digital footprint should represent your future, not your mistakes. It should reflect your goals, your character, and your growth. You can be funny, expressive, and creative, but also be smart about what you share.

Think before you post. Protect your name, protect your future, and protect your peace.

Your social media is your digital résumé. Treat it like your reputation depends on it because it does.

Reflection Questions:
- What message does your social media send about you right now?
- Have you ever deleted a post because you realized it did not represent you well?
- How can you use your online platforms to build instead of destroy?
- What would future you think about what you post today?

Your digital footprint shows how the world sees you, but self-development is how you see yourself. What you post might build your image, but what you learn and practice builds your future. The next chapter focuses on that inner work, the daily investment in becoming a better, stronger version of you.

CHAPTER 16: SELF-DEVELOPMENT

"All the school kids are so sick of books and learning; they don't read anymore" Drake

Self-development is making an investment in yourself. It is the commitment to improve every area of your life. It can include discipline, reading, fitness, spiritual growth, education, and finances. Self-development is the foundation that builds the person you are becoming and want to become. You cannot always control circumstances, but you can control your preparation and your effort. Every day is an opportunity to pour something back into yourself.

For me, self-development means staying in competition with myself. It is Me vs. Me. I am not chasing another man's goals, money, or success. I am chasing the version of me that is one step ahead, the version that already learned the lesson, ran the extra mile, and made the better decision. I do not need motivation from anyone else. I have already seen what happens when I stay consistent, and that alone fuels me.

I realized how important self-development was when I started college. Before that, my focus was mostly physical, running faster, lifting heavier, staying fit. But when I went back to school while serving in the Army, something changed. I wanted to be sharper mentally, not just physically. At that point in my life, I wanted to become a better version of myself for my daughter.

College flipped a switch in my mind. I learned how to think critically, communicate clearly, and organize my thoughts through writing. I had no idea how much writing could separate good from great until I watched people struggle with it. In the Army, effective communication can make or break a mission. A lot can get lost in translation if something is not fully communicated. College taught me how to communicate efficiently.

I remember taking a course while in the Army that required a lot of writing, and a pattern developed right in front of me. The Soldiers who struggled the most were the ones whose highest level of education was high school. That experience taught me something simple but powerful: education is growth. Every time you learn something new, you sharpen your tools for life.

Self-development is not just reading books or sitting in classrooms. It is learning from life itself. For example, I once decided I wanted to cook for my family instead of just ordering food. I watched videos, read cookbooks, practiced recipes, and messed up plenty of meals. But eventually, I started understanding flavor and timing. Now my kids love when I cook, but they have no idea how many bad dinners it took to get there. That is self-development in action, the behind-the-scenes work no one sees.

Growth looks like that in every area of life. It is unglamorous, repetitive, and sometimes lonely. You fail, learn, adjust, and try again. Over time, those small efforts add up. You look back one day and realize you have outgrown the person you used to be.

People stunt their growth when they stop searching for answers. They settle for comfort instead of curiosity. They scroll instead of study. They compare instead of commit. Too many people want success faster than they want to understand it.

If you want to grow, you have to feed your mind. Read. Research. Ask questions. Listen to people who know more than you. Try things that scare you a little. And most importantly, apply what you learn. Reading a book without taking action is like buying gym clothes and never working out. The effort only counts when you move.

People misunderstand self-development because they think it is quick. They expect instant results. Real growth takes time. It is slow, quiet, and sometimes frustrating. There will be days when you wonder if the work is even worth it. But it is. Progress rarely announces itself. It builds in the background while you are consistent. Months later, someone else might notice before you do.

I have learned that growth requires patience. You have to trust the process even when it feels like nothing is happening. Think about how a seed grows underground before breaking through the dirt. That is self-development. Everything starts beneath the surface before the results ever show.

Making time for self-development is non-negotiable. Life will always offer distractions, but growth never happens by accident. You have to make time for it. We make time for social media, games, and entertainment, so we can make time to improve. Read ten pages before bed. Listen to an educational podcast while you drive. Use your lunch break to research something that interests you. It does not have to be a huge change; it just has to be consistent.

Sometimes people say, "I just don't have time." I tell them, you have time, you just do not have structure. Time will disappear if you do not tell it where to go. When you schedule growth, you get results.

The hardest part of self-development is accepting that growth can hurt. It is not always fun. It might mean letting go of people who do not want to grow with you. It might mean spending weekends alone studying or practicing while everyone else is out. It might mean feeling uncomfortable because you are challenging yourself in new ways. But pain is the price of progress. Growth and comfort do not live in the same space. And that is okay. Everything you sacrifice to grow eventually comes back multiplied in confidence, skill, peace, and opportunities. Every version of yourself requires a new level of work but also rewards you with a new level of understanding.

Self-development connects to everything else in this book. Your why gives you purpose. Your character defines your integrity. Your ambition provides direction. Your discipline keeps you consistent. Your circle keeps you accountable. Your peace gives you space to breathe. But self-development ties it all together. It ensures you never stop improving.

This journey is not about perfection. It is about intention. Every step you take toward growth matters. Even reading this book is part of your development. You cared enough about your future to look for guidance, and that alone puts you ahead of the crowd.

Self-development is not a phase. It is a lifestyle. You will never be done working on yourself, and that is a beautiful thing. The goal is not to become flawless; the goal is to stay hungry. Every book you read, every skill you learn, every risk you take adds another layer to who you are.

You are your greatest project. Every experience, lesson, and challenge is shaping the person you are becoming. Keep investing in that person.

Reflection Questions:
- What is one area of your life you want to develop right now?
- Who can you learn from that you have not reached out to yet?
- How can you challenge yourself to step outside your comfort zone this month?

Growth will expose you to new environments, new people, and new opportunities. You will find yourself in rooms you once only dreamed of. In those moments, it is easy to start blending in, to adjust your identity just to fit the setting. Real growth is not about changing who you are to match your surroundings. It is about being confident enough to evolve and bring your true self wherever you go.

CHAPTER 17: STAY TRUE TO YOURSELF

"Win From Within!"

Staying true to yourself is one of the hardest things to do in a world that constantly tries to shape you. Life has a way of testing your identity. The higher you climb, the more pressure you feel to fit in, to adjust, or to become someone you are not. Success means nothing if you lose yourself in the process.
Who you are, your beliefs, values, and character, is what makes you unique. It is what got you this far. Every chapter in this book has focused on discipline, consistency, resilience, and growth. But this final chapter is a reminder that none of it matters if you forget who you are at your core. Growth is powerful, but authenticity is what keeps you grounded.

I have developed and evolved over time, but I have always remained myself. I am a kid from Augusta, Georgia, trying to make my parents proud. No matter how far I go, I will never forget that! That is me. That is my background. That is my story.

Being myself is what carried me this far. I never needed to pretend to be something else to achieve success. The more authentic I became, the more confidence I gained. The more I stayed rooted in my identity, the easier it became to lead, to communicate, and to inspire.

We all evolve over time, and we should. Growth is a natural part of life. But evolution does not mean abandoning your foundation. You can expand, improve, and mature without losing the core of who you are. Growth should elevate your identity, not erase it.

I have watched people reinvent themselves the moment life challenges them or their financial situation changes. They conform their identity for what they believe others expect. They let go of their values to blend into a new environment. But once you disconnect from your foundation, it becomes harder to recognize yourself. Your character becomes unclear, and your direction becomes unstable.

Authenticity is not perfection. It is honesty. It is being aware of your strengths and your weaknesses. Accept your weaknesses and work on them. Accept your strengths and do not neglect them. Confidence is not arrogance. Confidence is awareness. It is knowing what you bring to the table and standing on it no matter the room you walk into.

Be proud of how you were raised. Be proud of your story. Your struggles, your setbacks, your wins, and your experiences shaped the person you are today. The values you were given—respect, discipline, honesty, humility—are the same values that will carry you farther than any position or paycheck ever could. Live those values daily.

Staying true to yourself also means recognizing your wants and needs. Too often, people chase an image of success instead of pursuing a life that actually fulfills them. You do not need to prove anything to anyone. You do not need to match anyone's timeline. Your life is your own. Build it in a way that makes sense to you, not to the opinions of others.

It is easy to start performing for approval. You change your voice, your habits, your style, or your goals to match the expectations of others. But with each adjustment, you drift further away from the person you truly are. Over time, that distance creates confusion. You feel lost not because you lack purpose, but because you stepped away from your identity. Staying true to yourself is not just a choice, it is a discipline. It keeps you connected to your purpose.

When I look at my own journey, I do not see someone who changed. I see someone who evolved. My patience improved, my leadership strengthened, and my goals became clearer. But at the core, I am still Nigel from Augusta. The same drive that pushed me years ago is the same drive that keeps me focused today. If I want to continue to win from within, I have to protect the foundation that built me.

People will come and go. Opinions will shift. Environments will change. Trends will fade. Your values and your identity are yours to protect. They are your internal compass when everything around you becomes unfamiliar. When life pulls you in different directions, return to who you are and why you started. That is what keeps you grounded.

Your experiences shape how you see the world. Let them guide you, but do not let them harden you. The goal is not to become unrecognizable; it is to become undeniable. Growth should make you stronger, wiser, and more prepared. It should not make you abandon the person who began the journey. Learn from life, but never lose sight of the person living it.

The beauty of staying true to yourself is that it makes every achievement more meaningful. When you succeed without sacrificing your integrity, you feel proud because the accomplishment is genuine. You earned it by staying authentic. No pretending. No performing. Just growth.

Your journey will bring highs and lows, wins and setbacks, clarity and confusion. But staying true to yourself will always bring you back to center. That is how you win from within. Success begins with you, and it lasts when you remain aligned with your identity.

Reflection Questions
- What values define me?
- Where have I evolved, and where have I drifted from who I am?
- How can I continue to grow without losing myself?

Be proud of who you are. Embrace where you came from. Continue to evolve, but never forget the foundation that built you. Your authenticity, your values, and your truth will always be your greatest strength. Carry them forward with confidence and remember that growth never stops. The moment you get comfortable, you stop becoming your best self.

REFLECTION: NEVER GET COMFORTABLE

"You're only as big as your last accomplishment."

You are only as big as your last accomplishment. This is not meant to be harsh; it is a reminder to keep growing.

Graduating high school is great, but it is something you are supposed to do. Getting your first job, earning a promotion, buying your first car—those are all steps, not finish lines. The mistake people make is treating milestones like destinations. The moment you stop improving, you start regressing.

The job is not over. Growth is a lifelong assignment, not a temporary project. Every goal you reach should prepare you for the next one. The reward for hard work is not rest; it is the opportunity to do more, become more, and give more.

Complacency is the silent killer of dreams. The moment you believe you have arrived, you stop striving for what is next. True growth lives in the space between who you are and who you are becoming.

Comfort is one of the biggest threats to progress. It sneaks up quietly, disguised as stability. You get comfortable with your routine, your paycheck, your circle, and before you know it, years have passed and nothing has changed. Never confuse being comfortable with being fulfilled.

Be proud, but stay humble.

Be satisfied, but stay hungry.

Be grateful, but never stop growing.

Every season demands a new version of you. The lessons that carried you this far will need updating, and that is a good thing. Keep adjusting, keep sharpening, and keep becoming.

Your story is not over. Every win gives you momentum, but only if you use it to move forward.

Celebrate your accomplishments, but do not live in them.

Because you are only as big as your last one.

FINAL SUMMARY

Success does not happen overnight. It takes time, focus, and consistency. Everything we covered in this book comes down to one thing: you.

You learned that success starts from within, but it continues through character, ambition, and discipline. You learned to read the room, know your audience, protect your circle, and manage your time. You learned that failure is not the end; it is part of the process. Every mistake, every setback, every long night is building you into who you are meant to be.

You learned to protect your peace, choose your circle wisely, and understand that who you surround yourself with can shape your direction. You learned to show up with presence and confidence. You saw that appearance matters, but true growth happens beneath the surface.

You learned that time is currency, your digital footprint represents your character, and that self-development never stops. The journey to success is constant learning, refining, and becoming a better version of yourself each day.

Your growth will not always be loud. Sometimes it happens in silence, when no one is watching. But those are the moments that shape you. Stay grounded, stay consistent, and remember your "why".

You are the foundation of your own success. No mentor, no opportunity, and no shortcut can replace the work you put in daily. When you master your mindset, everything else begins to align.

Success is not a finish line; it is a lifestyle.

Keep showing up.

Keep improving.

Keep developing.

Keep winning from within.

Win from within.

Success starts with you.

A NOTE TO THE READER

Thank you for taking the time to invest in yourself.

Writing this book was more than sharing lessons. It was about reminding you that growth is personal, and progress begins the moment you decide to start.

There will be days when motivation fades, and discipline is all you have. Those are the days that define you. Keep showing up. Keep putting in the work, even when it is quiet, even when no one is watching.

You do not need perfection. You need persistence. Every step forward counts, no matter how small it feels.

Take what you have learned here and apply it to your daily life. Revisit these pages whenever you need a reminder of who you are becoming.

The next chapter of your life is waiting on your action, not your permission.

Keep going.

ABOUT THE AUTHOR

Nigel Norvell is a dedicated leader, author, and lifelong advocate for personal growth. Originally from Augusta, Georgia, he has spent his career inspiring others to reach their full potential through self-discipline, education, and consistent effort. Nigel believes that true success begins from within and that personal development is a daily decision to improve in every area of life.

As the founder of Books By Norvell, he has created a growing collection of children's books that blend strength, family, and purpose. His stories are designed to motivate the next generation while encouraging parents to lead by example.

Through both his children's series and Win From Within: Success Starts With You, Nigel's mission remains the same: to help others invest in themselves, embrace growth, and win the battles that matter most.